Learning
Without
Boundaries

How to Make Virtual Schooling Work for You™

CONNECTIONS ACADEMY®

Baltimore, Maryland

Contents

What is a Virtual School? 4

How to Make Virtual Schooling Work for You 5

    Classroom Set-Up. 7

    Time Management. 13

    Motivation Strategies. 18

    Reward Systems. 24

    Managing Multiple Students. 29

    Curriculum Planning. 36

    Students with Special Challenges. 42

    Using Technology. 46

    Integrating the Roles of Parent and Coach 52

    Extra Credit. 57

Connections Academy Success Stories 63

Glossary 79

Copyright© 2004 by Connections Academy®, LLC.

All rights reserved. This book has been reproduced using content provided by Connections Academy® families and employees. Connections Academy has been granted the rights to publish this content. No part of these materials may be reproduced or transmitted in any form or by any means without permission in writing from Connections Academy. The Connections Academy name and logo are trademarks of Connections Academy, LLC. Power Point is a trademark of Microsoft Corporation. All rights reserved. Any use of any of these marks without the expressed written consent of the owner of the mark is strictly prohibited.

ISBN 0-9763685-0-1

What is a Virtual School?

These are exciting times for parents, teachers, and others who believe that each and every child should receive a personalized education that recognizes his or her unique abilities and interests. This is a time when education isn't limited to a time of the day; when students who can move ahead, or those who need more help don't have to wait for the rest of the group or feel the pain of being left behind. It's a time when the unique knowledge of the parents and caregivers who know their children best is not left at home, but is integrated into a program to help develop the knowledge and values that will shape these children and follow them into adulthood. Why is this happening now?

Technology is changing education by enabling innovative thinkers to create public schools that are virtual. They are not defined by their space, but by their learning program and mission. Computers and the Internet enable these schools to deliver instruction, monitor progress, assess performance and facilitate communication between parents, students, teachers, and administrators – not only on a local level, but with others across the country.

Technology alone does not make virtual schools successful. It is the families and educators who create and define them. But in a school without walls, the parents are truly partners with the teachers and administrators. And today, they are pioneers in developing the best practices that will help other families to succeed in this new form of public school.

We are fortunate to have a dynamic group of parents who were willing to share their ingenuity, creativity, and enthusiasm to create this book. I want to thank everyone who submitted an idea or a story to us, and regret that we could not include them all. I also appreciate all of the hard work of our teachers and principals, along with everyone in our educational and marketing staff who made this book a reality.

If you are joining the Connections Academy family, we welcome you and hope that the ideas in this book will help you and your children create a memorable and successful school year. For some, success means returning a child next year to the local bricks-and-mortar school; for others, it's committing to virtual schooling for the long-term. We hope that you will find inspiration and encouragement from other families who have made this decision and seen it change their lives. And many of these suggestions will be useful for your family, regardless of what kind of schooling you use.

Refer to the last page of the book for more about our program.

From our family to your family, all the very best,

Barbara J. Dreyer

President, Connections Academy

How to Make Virtual Schooling Work for You

Creating a Successful Learning Environment at Home

Each day, the parents and students in our program find creative ways to make learning in a home (or other non-classroom) environment work for their unique situations. We are always impressed with the solutions they devise to overcome challenges. In this book, we've compiled some of the best recommendations our families have to offer. We hope that what you learn here will help your own students achieve their full potential. While some of the suggestions are specific to the Connections Academy program,* many of them are useful for families who are homeschooling or who are providing their children with extra help at home while they're attending a traditional public school.

*See Glossary on Page 79 for descriptions of Connections Academy terminology used throughout the book.

Classroom Set-Up: Ideas for use of space, filing assignments, organizing textbooks, and special classroom features

Time Management: Helpful hints on structuring the school day, coordinating outside activities or appointments, handling unexpected interruptions, scheduling, and planning

Motivation Strategies: Advice for motivating students, overcoming difficult academic challenges, instilling self-discipline, goal-setting, and character formation

Reward Systems: Suggestions for rewarding academic progress, meeting deadlines, reaching specific goals, and a good attitude

Managing Multiple Students: Pointers on how to juggle Learning Coach demands, handling sibling comparisons and competition, and scheduling one-on-one time

Curriculum Planning: Recommendations for short- and long-range planning, how to streamline assignments, tips for portfolio assignments, taking advantage of the Personalized Learning Plan, and modifying lessons to address individual needs

Students with Special Challenges: Guidance on modifying the curriculum, strategies for building self-esteem, keeping goals realistic, dividing tasks into increments, maintaining a positive attitude, and the best advantages of a virtual setting

Using Technology: How to take advantage of the most helpful features of the Learning Management System, getting comfortable with technology, and working with our technology support department

Integrating the Roles of Parent and Coach: Information on establishing a disciplined and joyful household, setting ground rules, scheduling chores for the kids, and the importance of tapping into support systems

Extra Credit: Anything not covered by the first nine categories!

When you see this icon, you'll know this tip came from a Connections Academy staff member.

Classroom Set-Up

Integrating a classroom into a home can be a challenge, so we asked our families to give us tips on classroom set-up, including ideas on the use of space, filing assignments, organizing textbooks, and special classroom features.

Use your workspace effectively to contribute to academic success.

- Designate a special area just for your student.

- If your child is a visual learner, have plenty of bright colorful highlighters ready for use in a brightly colored cup or pencil holder.

- Purchase inexpensive stack file racks at an office supply store and label them with the name of each subject your child is studying.

- Purchase novelty pencils that are fun and interesting to your student, and they will motivate her to pick them up and use them.

- When you finish a Portfolio assignment, label it with the lesson number and file it in a separate folder. Then it is ready to go when the time comes to mail in all the Portfolio assignments.

- Purchase a monitor stand that allows the keyboard to slide under the monitor and out of the way when not in use.

- Use a dry erase board to display the day's assignments and allow the student to check them off as he or she finishes them.

- Use a corkboard to display lengthy assignments and artwork.

- Let your child pick out a comfortable student chair in his or her favorite color.

- The Learning Coach should have his or her own space. Set up a desk in close proximity to the student's.

- Stay in the room with your student. This allows the student to ask questions and gives you the ability to assess the student's knowledge.

The Antolocis organize their workspace for maximum efficiency.

- Buy posters that follow the curriculum and display them in the work area.
- Assess your learning area monthly since students need changes of scenery to keep them engaged. (KarenKay Antoloci, OH)

 **TIP:** Send a picture of your student to the teacher. It really helps to put a face with the name and creates a sense of community.

Keep materials handy.

We like to use one large five-subject notebook rather than searching for a lot of little notebooks. We also put all of our writing tools in a bright orange plastic pumpkin next to the computer. It's now easier to start our writing assignments each day, and we also have a silly jack-o-lantern face watching our progress. (Cheryl Tollestrup, AZ)

The Tollestrups integrate fun into their learning.

Plan ahead.
Each of our girls has a desk with an in/out box on it. We place their assignments for the next day in the in box the evening before, which keeps us at least a day ahead in looking over their lessons. This also means that the girls can see what to expect for the next day and they have the option of getting some of their work out of the way the night before. They also know to place their finished work in the out box. This keeps interruptions down if you're working with another student. (Barbara and Dwayne Drury, FL)

TIP: Occasionally take class outside on nice days. Students might use this change of scenery as inspiration for their writing journals, and they can be challenged to find creative ways to incorporate nature into their daily lessons.

Allow for personalization.
Creating areas where students can keep their books and supplies helps them with discipline and makes them more self-sufficient. It's also nice if the student can make it his "own" by decorating it himself. (Kristi and Phil Harms, WI)

The Harms students personalize their work areas.

Be creative.
We built large cubbies, one for each child, with a desk and shelves to hold books and the family reading library. The cubbies are hidden by folding closet doors, and when the doors are shut school disappears from view. (John and Carol Meyer, CO)

Use sticky notes and tabs.
We use sticky tabs to mark pages in textbooks that need to be read, and use the notes to let our student know what is required on certain assignments. This helps him do his work more expeditiously because he has direction. Each night, our student is required to clean his desk so he can start each new day ready for school. (Leah and Robert Sandoval, CO)

Each day starts with a clean desk in the Sandoval home.

TIP: Attach clips to a strip of wood and mount the strip on a wall in your classroom area. Use this to display artwork and assignments of which the student is proud. The clips allow the student to change the items on a regular basis.

TIP: The learning area does not have to be all in one room – you can set up computers in one room, desks in another.

Divide materials into groups.

The materials you use on a regular basis can be divided into three groups: textbooks; computer and components; and lesson plans, files, and notebooks. The textbooks are best kept on a bookshelf next to your work area. The computer and components fit well on a large work table with a roll-out keyboard and mouse drawer. The table provides enough room for the student to work on lesson plans, etc. The assignments, Portfolio, and notebooks should be placed in a filing cabinet or simple box. The Portfolio folder should be placed at the front of the box or cabinet with items inside in preparation for mailings to the teacher. (John and Roxanne Mesyk, WI)

The Mesyks use a large work table at the center of their learning area.

Invent your own tools.

We have used the backs of doors for everything. We attached a dry erase board to the top half and used magnetic paint for the bottom half to turn it into a magnet board. On the very top of the door, you can attach a roller shade and then apply maps, the alphabet, etc. Use a clothespin bag to hold various other supplies for the boards. (Jesika and David Moses, WI)

Be flexible.
I keep our books in a rolling set of plastic drawers. There is a drawer for each child and it keeps the books accessible yet out of sight. I can roll the cabinet into the closet when we need the books out of the way. (Katherine Sanderson, WI)

Make it easy for the kids to find things.
We have a large bookshelf that is used exclusively for school books and supplies and my children can go there to find anything they need for their assignments. On those shelves, we divided the items into baskets, and each basket has a label on it so that we know what it contains (e.g., Science equipment and supplies or writing materials). Each child also has a large colored crate with his or her name on it where all the books they use on a daily basis are kept. (Jane Kummer-Meyer and Robert Meyer, WI)

TIP: It is important that students feel ownership of the design and layout of their learning area. Hold occasional "meetings" with your students to discuss improvements that can be made.

Connections Academy students take a break from their studies.

Classroom Set-Up

Time Management

One of the biggest advantages to schooling your child in a non-traditional setting is the flexibility of scheduling, but students are still responsible for managing their time in a responsible way. Our families shared ideas on structuring the school day or week, coordinating outside activities or appointments, handling unexpected interruptions, and using the Connections Academy Scheduler.

Free time is important to the Garcia family.

Arrange your schedule with extracurricular activities in mind.

If your child wants to go somewhere special or has an appointment scheduled, have her do two days' worth of work in one day so she will have free time to enjoy. Or, if you feel that your child has too many subjects in one day, you can easily rearrange your Scheduler and give you and your child a break. If she wants to go on a field trip and can get done with work very quickly, then have her do half the lessons before the trip and the rest after. (Raisa Garcia, PA)

Let your child help guide the schedule.

I realized that as a mom who schools at home, I do need to have a schedule, but the schedule is not set in stone. One of the greatest assets of schooling at home is the flexibility. If my daughter wants to read four chapters in one day, that's great. If she really comprehends the Math, we can do three lessons in one day. If she feels imaginative, we can complete two writing assignments. If she has "writer's block" we can skip Writing for that day and do it the next day. If she's struggling with the Math assignment, we can go over it for two or three days until she understands the concept. I have found that by allowing my daughter's attitude to guide our schedule, we have stayed on track, completed the required studies, and developed a bond that would not be there if I sent her to traditional school. (Carolyn Startzell, AZ)

TIP: If a child is having a hard time understanding a concept, move on to a different subject and return to it later. This helps keep both the Learning Coach and the student from becoming too frustrated. Teachers in traditional classrooms frequently use this learning tactic.

A flexible schedule works for the Startzells.

Use egg timers to help you stay on task.
Children learn different subjects at different rates. Once you develop a sense of your student's learning style and pace, set goals for the amount of time it should take to complete each lesson, and set a timer accordingly. Reward your child with a break if he gets done before the egg timer goes off. Even if the timer goes off before he is finished with a subject, go to the next subject and assign the rest as homework. This has helped our son develop a sense of time management and to focus on the subject. Now he is self-disciplined enough not to need the timer. (Dan and Marcie Mulligan, PA)

Help your child establish a routine.
For some families a flexible learning schedule works best, but for us a regular routine keeps us on track. We set a schedule for our school day with a consistent start time, lunch time and dismissal time. As hard as it is, we start the same time every day. Otherwise we might easily start a habit of sleeping in and then be frustrated when schoolwork isn't done. Any work not finished by dismissal time is considered homework and cuts into our son's playtime. (Dan and Marcie Mulligan, PA)

Science is fun for the DeLongs.

TIP: Increments of time can be a difficult concept for young children to grasp. Begin teaching students about time management at a young age by talking about things happening in seconds, minutes, hours, days, months and years. Then discuss your student's learning schedule and how much time will be spent on each activity. This helps the student to actively participate in keeping on track with the day's schedule.

Do something school-related every day.
The biggest thing we learned this year is to make sure we do at least one school-related activity every day. It can be tempting to take a day or two off, causing you to fall behind. Then you have to play catch up. This isn't fun for the Learning Coach or the student. (Robin Hertting, WI)

Share your schedule with family and friends.
Our goal is to start the school day by 8 a.m. The boys get up early, take care of family responsibilities, and eat breakfast. We work until 11 a.m. and then have an early lunch followed by a break. For the morning to be successful, school has to be our priority. We also have communicated our morning school routine to friends and family and they are respectful of our school focus during that time. We don't answer the phone unless it's a teacher from Connections Academy. In the morning, we usually do subjects that require the Learning Coach's involvement and the afternoon subjects might be writing assignments that can be worked on with less help. This allows the Learning Coach the opportunity to multitask and return a phone call, perform some household responsibilities, prep for dinner, or check other assignments in the afternoon. We also use the Connections Academy Scheduler to assign fewer lessons two days a week, Tuesday and Thursday. That allows us to schedule appointments or other activities on those days. (John and Carol Meyer, CO)

The Mackins enjoy a school field trip.

Help your kids stick to a schedule.
We have found that sticking to a schedule is important. I spend an hour per child on the weekend going over lesson plans and writing out schedules for each of my children. This really helps with time management during the week. Fridays usually end up being our light days. This motivates my children and they have stayed on schedule. (Ashlee Harris, CO)

TIP: Be realistic about the time it takes to complete tasks. Not all students work at the same speed, and not all subjects require the same amount of time. Adjust your student's schedule accordingly.

Motivation Strategies

Our families have developed many of their own strategies for keeping their students excited about learning. Here they share ideas for overcoming difficult academic challenges, instilling self-discipline, goal-setting, character formation, and developing independence.

Use games to make learning fun.

Each morning I post a "Brain Teaser" question on our classroom's dry erase board. This question covers any subject matter we currently are studying. My son can attempt an answer to this question before our school day actually begins. This draws him to the classroom and motivates him to get started on our school day.

I have found this question to serve several purposes. It can act as a review of a subject we covered the day before, which is helpful in preparing for quizzes and tests. Secondly, it acts as an introduction of a concept to see what my student already knows and understands, so I can tailor my instruction to his present understanding of a subject or topic. This saves time and keeps the student interested and motivated to learn. (Kathy R. Pasch, PA)

Brain Teasers motivate in the Pasch household.

TIP: Schedule some time during the week for fun educational activities. For example, visit a museum, the zoo, or the aquarium on a Tuesday, when these attractions are much less crowded. Plan trips around what the kids are learning in their courses.

Use Marble Jars.

We use a system for motivation we call the "Marble Jars." Each of our students has been given his own clear jar that each day is filled with as many marbles as there are lessons for the day. Each student also has an empty "completed" jar as well. Every time an assignment is completed, he may remove one marble and place it in the completed jar. When the start jar is empty, the school day is completed. We insist that the start jar is empty before the kids are allowed to play. This is very helpful when one of my students is having difficulty with a particular subject or lesson. This method also has been very helpful with one of our students who has Sensory Integration Dysfunction because she is much calmer when she can actually "see" how much she has to accomplish during the day. (Candice Presley-Weakland, FL)

Involve your children in your community.

Our children volunteer twice a week at a local veterinary clinic. The clinic experience is one they truly enjoy, but they may go only if schoolwork is done well and attitudes are appropriate. Their experience at the clinic helps in many ways. It motivates them in their schoolwork, is a reward for work well done, provides social interaction in a quality environment, develops mature responses from them, provides experience in life sciences and introduces them to the wide world of community volunteering. (John and Carol Meyer, CO)

A student's artwork decorates a window.

Find a special place to display schoolwork.
Have one section of your wall just for schoolwork pages, whether it's art, handwriting that your student worked really hard to make neat, or a test that was difficult. Have a place to hang some of the things that are returned from the teacher so your student can see that the teacher does look at her assignments and the rest of the family can see what she's working on. It gives her a big boost of confidence that is needed on a tough day. (Anna Weir, PA)

TIP: Reverse roles. Have the student create a quiz for the Learning Coach to take. Children love trying to stump their parents. Have students teach a lesson to the Learning Coach. This reinforces the material and shows the student how much work is involved in preparing a lesson.

Make personal journals a family keepsake.
Once a week or so, the girls had an assignment of writing a personal journal entry. They each chose a special notebook that they used for this assignment and they always dated their entries. Now we have a school year's collection of thoughts, activities, and feelings that were important to them at this age, and we are sure they will enjoy looking back on these for years to come. (I know we will!) (Larry and Nancy Kremer, WI)

TIP: Play games with spelling words throughout the week. Go outside and write words with sidewalk chalk, write on the bathroom mirror with shaving cream or soap, or hide the words on slips of paper throughout the house in unexpected places.

Find special activities that motivate your child to learn.
My son was having a hard time learning spelling words in our classroom. He just wasn't getting it. One evening he picked up the jump rope we use for Physical Education, asked me a spelling word, and jumped as he spelled it out. (Who would have thought?) So, his favorite way to learn spelling words is to go outside and jump rope. I sit in a chair with a stack of spelling cards and call them out to him. He spells out each word by jumping and saying each letter of that word. (Sami Platter, FL)

Let your child see his progress.
Review where your child started a week, month, or year ago and compare it with his current abilities. This helps him see what he has accomplished and develop goals. Write down goals with your child and post them so he can check them off as they're done. (Sundae Benton, CO)

The Bentons chart their goals.

Combine learning with play.

The children play a basketball game called HORSE in our driveway. Now, we use spelling words to play. They each take a turn trying to make a basket, calling out a letter if they make it. If the shot is missed, they re-shoot the ball, then call out the letter for that particular word.

We keep lots of sidewalk chalk around our house. Our children love to draw on our driveway with it, so I sit outside with them and give each a spelling word. They can draw pictures only if they spell the word correctly on our driveway. At the end of our lesson, they get to clean the driveway with water and also soak each other with the hose. (Sami Platter, FL)

TIP: Encourage the student to be creative when coming up with ideas for his or her journal. Ideas could be anything from "My favorite day" to "Describe something in the room" to "What it would be like to be an animal for a day." Write each idea on a slip of paper, fold the paper, and put the folded slips in a bag. When it comes time to write a journal entry, the student picks a slip from the bag and starts writing on that topic. This helps move the writing process along by turning it into a game.

Motivation Strategies

"Fun" lessons are a reward for students in the DeLong household.

Start with the least favorite lesson first.

This motivates my children to keep studying because they are always working towards the activities and lessons they most enjoy. After breakfast, sit together and talk without hurrying, discuss the day and set goals together. Have a schedule, but be flexible. When evaluating some of our most stressful days of learning, I usually find lack of communication resulted in frustration for all of us. (Tammy DeLong, FL)

 **TIP:** Some students find it rewarding to watch the Learning Coach mark off the assignments as they are completed.

Reward Systems

For many students, learning is its own reward. But some students need an extra push. Many of our students respond well to rewards that acknowledge academic progress, meeting deadlines, reaching specific goals, and good attitudes.

Students learn money management skills in the Law household.

Use money jars to teach good money management skills.

We have our children divide the money they receive into six categories and create a jar for each one. All rewards go into the money jars as follows: future financial account jar for building wealth; an education jar for things such as books, tapes, and classes; a give jar for tithing and donations; a long-term savings-to-spend jar for big-ticket items; a play jar for entertainment money which must be used in full each month; and a necessities jar to pay for snacks or for older kids to pay for part of an activity.

The jars help the children develop self-discipline, character, and independence by creating a structured way of setting goals, and gets them in the habit of good money management skills. (Kim Law, FL)

 **TIP:** Free time is a big motivator for students. Keep a chart during the week with 15-minute breaks listed. These can be given and taken away by the Learning Coach during the week. At appropriate times, the earned time can be "cashed in" by the student to do something he or she enjoys.

For competitive spirits, set up a point and reward system.

My daughter is a competitor! She is an award-winning gymnast and loves to win! I found that she needed goals to motivate her in her schoolwork just as she needs goals for herself at the gym. We set up a point and reward system at home to help her set and reach goals.

Make a chart with each school subject listed and a point value. Each day after my daughter completes her assignments, we sit down together and evaluate her attitude and the work completed in each subject area. If we both feel she has done a good job, she receives a point in that subject. If she had a bad attitude or other issues caused problems in completing a certain assignment, then no point is given in that subject. There is also a column for bonus points if she is having an exceptionally good day. Her points can never be taken away after she has earned them. Each week we tally up the points and keep a running total.

In addition to the "Points Chart" we have a "Rewards Chart." On the Rewards Chart there are various items listed that my daughter can "buy" with her points. For example, one item is a trip to the movies, popcorn included. She has to accumulate 80 points in order to "buy" this movie. Other items include staying up a half hour past regular bedtime, fixing mom's hair, and the biggie – a sleep-over party! My daughter has to decide how to spend her points, or if she wants to save them up for one of the "big ticket" items. Our motivation and reward system has made my job as a Learning Coach much easier. It gives my daughter some ownership and responsibility for her own learning. We are a great team! (Kris White, CO)

The end of a school day at the Sandoval house.

Create a tiered reward and discipline system.

We have a pyramid system that we use for both school time and home time. The pyramid has different levels of privileges. The bottom level is for bad behavior and involves having extra chores, no computer, and no television. The levels go up from there to full privileges and even a bonus area that would involve a special day alone with a parent. I place their designated peg on the level each child has achieved. The bonus area is achieved only through extra good deeds. The pyramid is our saving grace as it helps me to address my children's behavior in an objective manner. (Candice Presley-Weakland, FL)

TIP: Kids of all ages love charts and stickers. Make custom charts for both the student and Learning Coach that reflect their individual interests. Use the charts to track progress toward a goal, one each for the student and Learning Coach. Mark milestones as they are reached, and when the goal is achieved, give a reward related to the student's or Learning Coach's interest. Working on the charts together will motivate both parties.

The Durans head out for a break from school.

Use consistent rewards as motivation.
One of the best motivations for my son to get his work done every week is our special Friday afternoons. This is a consistent reward that I keep every week which has benefited the whole family because we all get to take a break from the house, school, and sometimes from each other. This has worked for us because it is something to look forward to each and every week. (Michelle Duran, CO)

Connections Academy students on a field trip to a museum.

Use big and small rewards.

Our reward system is based on "merit money." We purchased play money and covered it with contact paper to make it more durable. My children earn merit money which can be spent at the "Meyer Merit Market." I place a sticker on each item specifying the cost. There are items for as little as five merit dollars and some that are as high as fifty. This system encourages our children to work hard, but also teaches them the value of saving money and making good choices in their purchases. (Jane Kummer-Meyer and Robert Meyer, WI)

Turn learning itself into a reward.

One challenge we faced this year was teaching our child an ever-increasing list of new words. We could see his motivation waning as the pile of cards grew daily. After making a simple game of getting points for each word he pronounced correctly, he would remind us to let him play. The rules were that he would get one point for each word he sounded out correctly. We got one point for each word he missed, and there were some words that were marked on the back with bonus points. We found that playing the game was reward enough for him. If the other parts of the lesson went smoothly, he would earn the reward of playing "The Word Game." Our reward was watching his reading improve. (Maria and Greg Darby, CO)

Word games motivate in the Darby household.

Reward Systems

Managing Multiple Students

Many of our families have more than one student enrolled in the program. Managing multiple students requires additional curriculum preparation, but it also requires juggling Learning Coach demands and one-on-one time with each student. Comparison and competition issues can also arise between students in a small group setting.

Members of the Hughes family hard at work.

Plan ahead.
By planning ahead, I can see what each of my boys will be working on, and I've found that I can combine lessons and have them both work on the same subject or even on the same project. I make sure that the information from both lessons is included so that neither one of them misses anything. (Renee Hughes, AZ)

Schedule one-on-one, independent, and group activities.

We have two students and we divide their lessons and activities into three categories: one-on-one, independent, and group. While one student receives individual attention, the other works independently in a different room. In the afternoon, we do group lessons such as Art, Physical Education, Science experiments, or learning games. (Nancy and Mark Groszek, OH)

 **TIP:** Designate an area of the house as the "quiet zone" where students can retreat to work without distractions.

Allow students the opportunity to work independently.

I use a dry erase board and write each student's name with a list of activities he can complete on his own, such as technology class, spelling, writing, journaling, and tests. Then when I am working with another student on lessons, he can be getting some of his own schoolwork done. Deciding on the order in which he'll complete that work also gives him a feeling of independence. (Jean Pence, PA)

Creating time for independent study is important for the Pence family.

Managing Multiple Students

Create a system that will allow a student to work at his own pace without disrupting the day's schedule.

We have two students in the same grade and in order for the school day to be successful, they have to stay on relatively the same schedule. We start and close one subject before beginning the next. If one finishes before the other, we allow an appropriate completion time and then the remaining work goes into a scheduled homework slot. This helps the boys to stay focused on their work because they like to avoid homework.

We also have them check each other's work on certain assignments such as spelling and writing. This gives them a chance to see errors and to improve their proofreading skills. It also helps motivate them to do a good job because they don't want someone else finding their mistakes. On occasion, I have allowed them to do an assignment as a group project. This opportunity allows for a noncompetitive, positive experience of working with each other. (John and Carol Meyer, CO)

Each Meyer student works at his own pace.

TIP: If you have multiple students, teach lessons to one student during the other child's independent work time.

Give students their own space.

We originally did schoolwork together at the kitchen table. I thought my two daughters would learn better together, but the distractions were too great. Just looking at each other is enough to throw off the thought process. It is especially disruptive when the older child knows all the answers to the other child's work and calls it "easy."

Now each child works at a desk in her room. I go back and forth as needed. One child is not allowed to interrupt while I'm working with the other. If she finishes or gets stuck, she has something to read until I get back to her. The bedrooms are very close together and I notice right away if I'm needed in the other room. This has cut down tremendously on the breaks in concentration. I have also noticed that work gets done faster when one child is working alone with mom. (Barbara Drury, FL)

Give your students a chance to be empowered.

Our school day was almost always driven by the girls' choices. However, problems arose when their choices were in conflict with one another. To dispense with any counterproductive arguing, we gave one even-numbered days and the other odd-numbered days. On the respective days, each child took responsibility for choosing when to start the school day, in what order to do classes, when to call it quits for the day, and other decisions as necessary. The other child would agree knowing that the next day would be managed by her decisions. (Larry and Nancy Kremer, WI)

Managing Multiple Students

The Valentine students inspire one another by learning together.

Teach children to respect each other's time with the Learning Coach.

As we begin our day, we have both of the girls begin in the same subject, such as Math, so that they are working in the same "class period." This has worked very well, and they have learned how to work without talking out loud and disturbing each other. We feel that learning what it takes to give the other the space she needs is an integral part of the learning process.

Because our oldest girl was in a higher level of Math, this helped inspire our second grader, and she worked very diligently. We also had our spelling time together, and the girls enjoyed giving each other their spelling words for the tests. They knew not to give hints at how to spell the words, and when they were finished reading each other the lists of words they would hand their papers over to the Learning Coach for a spell check. (Maria and Jon Valentine, WI)

Create opportunities for students to mentor each other.

In our Connections Academy classroom we have four girls in three different grades. The girls are gymnasts and due to their morning gymnastics practice schedule, a traditional public school system doesn't work. So, our group of four moms decided to team-teach our four girls.

In our little classroom, the girls enjoy the luxury of working alone, with each other, and with different Learning Coaches depending on the day. As coaches we know our strengths and weaknesses and teach certain subjects based on our knowledge. Another advantage to our team approach is the ability to join in with projects and interesting lessons at different grade levels, including messy Science experiments in the kitchen.

The girls have found that they enjoy mentoring each other with this unique arrangement. The older girls frequently give spelling tests to the younger girls and reading aloud to each other has been beneficial for everyone. We've also used whiteboards to brainstorm ideas for essays and stories with all of the girls contributing suggestions. A map of the world has been a source of interesting discussions. We all now understand how an "open room school house" can function very efficiently and be beneficial to everyone. (Kris White, CO)

The Whites team up with other families for learning.

The Louwers family incorporates family vacations into their schooling.

TIP: To avoid interruptions, have a list ready for your students with things they can do while you are coaching other students.

Set physical boundaries.
I have our schoolroom and playroom set up in the same room with a low dividing wall so my younger children don't interrupt school as much, but still feel comfortable being near us. The dividing wall is made with two low bookshelves and a baby gate. (Christina Louwers, CO)

Curriculum Planning

The Connections Academy program allows for families to be creative in ways they work with the curriculum. Here they share ideas about short- and long-range planning, streamlining assignments, and taking advantage of customizing their child's education using the Personalized Learning Plan. Our parents also share tips on successful program modifications and communicating with teachers.

Pick topics of interest that motivate kids.

For one assignment, we selected four books (fiction, non-fiction, fantasy and poetry) related to one theme. Our eight-year-old son chose Native Americans and his activities included writing a story using Native American symbols, making a pair of moccasins using a kit, and making a map of various tribal lands in the United States. Our six-year-old son chose food as his theme and his activities included baking muffins and creating a menu for his own restaurant. These were fun to do and both boys were motivated to read more books on the chosen topic. (Nancy and Mark Groszek, OH)

Fun projects keep the Groszeks motivated.

TIP: Observe your student's learning style and interests. Then share your observations with the teacher to create your student's customized curriculum included in the Personalized Learning Plan.

Integrate the computer into your lessons.
Both our boys hate to write out their ideas but they love to type. So, after they complete the prewriting, drafting, editing, and revising steps in longhand, we let them use the computer to complete the final, published copy. They enjoy choosing the font type and size and using various software programs to illustrate their stories. They are proud of the final copy and see it as a reward for all their hard work. (Nancy and Mark Groszek, OH)

Create your own flashcards.
We use flashcards to study in a couple of different ways. We use the traditional way of putting questions on one side and answers on the other side, but we've also tried other study strategies. We play a matching game with the flashcards. The cards are shuffled and placed face-down on the table. On each child's turn, she turns up two cards. When she turns up a matching question and answer, she collects those two flashcards. The child with the most matching flashcards at the end is the winner. (Larry and Nancy Kremer, WI)

Prepare your lessons in advance.
In order to get all of our assignments completed, I would set out everything the night before that my daughter would need for the next day. If she had a spelling test I would print out a page that had her name, the date, and the unit she was testing for on the top, and then I would put the numbered lines down below the heading. This helped me keep track of the tests. (Shawn Johnston, CO)

Organizing lessons in advance keeps learning on track for the Johnstons.

Cut and paste.

Where there were questions in the assignments that needed to be answered I would highlight them on the computer page and copy and paste them to another document. I would then separate them enough so that there would be space to write the answers. This saved time because my daughter was not writing the questions and the answers, and I was not typing or writing the questions. I did this so that when it was time for the Portfolio assignments to be sent in we'd know exactly what each page was for. I would also add the top right corner description on the page and check it off of the Portfolio list. (Shawn Johnston, CO)

Use a visual list to keep on schedule.

In the beginning of the week, usually on Sundays, I will look through the agenda for the upcoming week. Hanging on the wall is a 2x3 foot dry erase board that I use to write an outline of what we'll be covering during the week. This usually contains a lot of the items that my boys can do on their own. (Susan VanWagner, FL)

TIP: Learning Coaches should look over lessons the night before and make notes that will help guide learning the next day.

Create an organizational system that works for you.

Connections Academy students write their name, the subject, the unit and lesson numbers, the title of the lesson, and the date at the top of each written assignment. I decided I would use my labeling software to streamline things a bit. I put all the required information on a label, and for the date, I just put in a line so my boys can write in the date. So I can find the label faster, I color code the text on the labels to correspond with each subject. (Susan VanWagner, FL)

Planning begins on Sunday for the VanWagners.

Watching the budget does not hinder creativity in the DeLong household.

Keep plenty of manila folders and gallon zip top bags handy.

When the curriculum arrives, I look over the scope and sequence for the year. Then I label the manila folders with the main topic themes and attach a gallon zip top bag to the front of each folder. They are designed for any additional resources I find on the subjects such as stickers, projects, field trip ideas, magazine articles, movies, etc. It takes a little more effort in the beginning to prepare the folders, but it sure does save time the rest of the year. (Tammy DeLong, FL)

A great place to find inexpensive supplemental resources is garage sales.

It also gets my children involved in the lessons by helping find projects and books they find interesting, as well as counting and budgeting money for the supplies. (Tammy DeLong, FL)

TIP: Use the Grade Book in the Learning Management System to keep track of lessons your student has completed and to monitor performance. The Grade Book provides an easy way to identify areas where your student excels and where additional attention is required.

Integrate family field trips into the learning process.

Take field trips that are related to the curriculum, such as attending concerts, and visiting art and science museums and historical sights, to give relevance to what your children are studying. Research museums prior to your visit because many offer low rates for families. Certain science museums and zoos belong to a national group that offers reciprocal memberships at other sites across the country. (Dan and Marcie Mulligan, PA)

The Mulligan students joined other Connections Academy families for a field trip at an amusement park.

Students with Special Challenges

Our teachers and Learning Coaches have found some inventive ways to work with this unique group of students. They've also gained great experience in initiating strategies for building self-esteem, keeping goals realistic, and dividing tasks into increments. Maintaining a positive attitude and leveraging the advantages of a virtual setting are also important for these students.

Sometimes learning is done on the couch in the Riesterer home.

Create an environment that suits your child's special needs.
My son has special attention problems and a language-based learning disability. Sitting at a table all day does not suit his learning style. He can pay attention so much better if I allow him to sit and bounce on a large exercise ball, hang upside down on the couch, or build Lego's while I read aloud. Then we sit still and read together for a period of time, or write, or do worksheets. We alternate these periods of activity with sitting still throughout the day. (Amy Riesterer, WI)

Support your special students with encouraging words.

My oldest daughter had fallen way behind in public school. She did not want to go back because she felt that she just "didn't get it." She felt inferior to her friends and her self-confidence and self-esteem were lacking. I sat by her, encouraging her, telling her she could do it even if it looked difficult. I also reminded her that it was okay to get it wrong because she could take an assignment over and over again if needed. I am happy to say that at the end of our year with Connections Academy my daughter is once again excited about going to school. She is at the level she should be. And most importantly, she has learned that if something looks difficult, try anyway. (Peggy Moore, CO)

TIP: Use only 10 spelling words at a time if 20 are too many.

Set realistic short-term and long-term goals.

Work with your child to set long- and short-term goals. We set long-term goals for a nine-week period and short-term goals for each day of the period. These goals have to be realistic so that the child with special needs does not get stressed out, but are not too easy to reach. We tie our goals to a reward system with simple prizes such as an extra hour of television or computer time, or bigger goals such as a new video game or book. (Norma Winings, CO)

Split lessons and tests into manageable sections.

My son struggles with writing and paying attention. After conferring with his teacher, we decided to present each written test question immediately following the lessons which covered that material. They were still difficult but not overwhelming because he can focus, finish, and move on. (Patti Shea, WI)

Find opportunities to teach each other.
My favorite modification, and the one with the best results, dealt with Geography. One day my son would read and study a chapter and I would do the same with the next chapter. The following day we would teach our respective chapters to each other with the help of the pictures in the text. This helped with quizzes and tests because I was certain that we had covered all the information. (Patti Shea, WI)

Learn to slow down.
My twins were working at a slower pace than expected. In reading, if they came across a word they were struggling with, I would count to five in my head. If they still hadn't decoded it, I would have them break it down by seeing if there was a familiar word in it, whether it was a compound word, or a word inside a word. I would then reinforce it by having them use it in a sentence and put it on the "word wall" until they felt comfortable with it. Knowing there are no time constraints, they seem to be more at ease. (Esther Milne, CO)

The Milne twins enjoy learning together.

Think outside the box.

My son's Attention Deficit Disorder makes it difficult for him to sit for a long time, and as a result, we do a lot of work while he walks around the room. He has boundaries (he must stay in the same room) but he gives much better answers because he is active. If he must sit in a chair, I wrap bungee straps around the front legs of the chair, which gives him something to "play" with. He's able to bounce his feet on them or put his feet behind them and pull his legs forward. (Annette Kranz, OH)

TIP: Learning Coaches should use consistent positive reinforcement to help students with low self-esteem issues.

Encouragement and a flexible schedule guide learning in the Moore household.

Using Technology

Technology has played a central role in the development of virtual schooling. Personal computers and the Internet now allow students and teachers to interact without being together in the same classroom. In a virtual school, technology enables parents to consult their child's teacher whenever necessary. Much of the advice in this section refers to Connections Academy's Learning Management System (LMS), but also applies to other technology tools.

Create a schedule that works for your family's lifestyle.

Use the LMS to make a lesson plan that works for your family. If you know you have a weekly activity (i.e. soccer practice, baseball, church, etc.) then schedule that into your calendar and schedule fewer subjects on those days. Or "block scheduling" (doing a week's worth of lessons in a day or two) might work better for your family. I like block scheduling especially for Art and Science because you can pull everything out that you need at one time instead of three or four times in a week. Or, if the traditional schedule of Monday through Friday does not work for your family, you can schedule subjects on Saturday, Sunday and holidays.

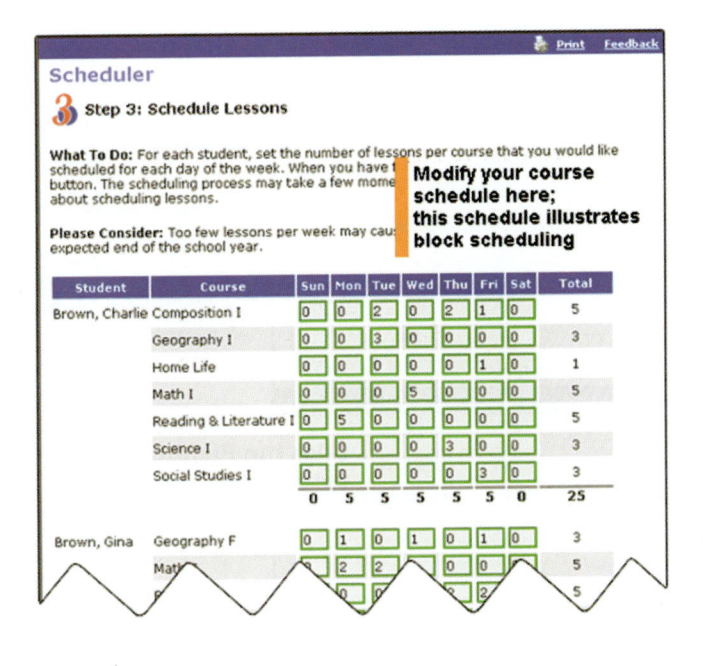

Try it one way, and if that doesn't work, try another. Each student is an individual and learns differently. Do what is best for you and your student. (Peggy Moore, CO)

TIP: Where does this go? When you don't know what an icon does, just put your mouse over it and wait a few seconds. A description of the icon's function will appear.

Monitor your child's progress every day.

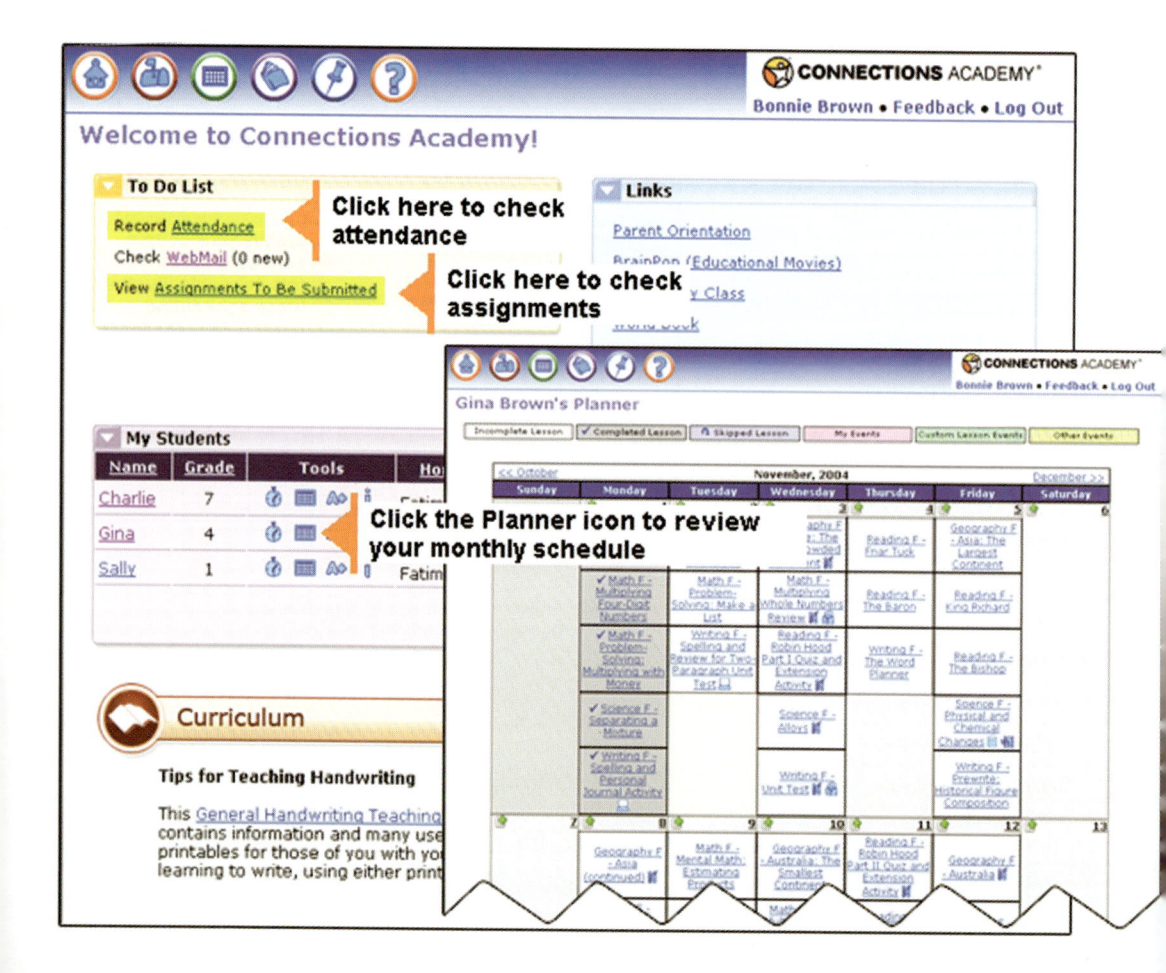

When you first log in to the system, check off your attendance and review the list of assignments. Check off the work that has been completed immediately after you have reviewed the assignment with your child so that you do not have an excess of overdue assignments. Look ahead at the whole month's schedule with your child so that you are not overwhelmed at the end of the month by assignments you didn't complete. Take time during the day or at least every other day to look at the message boards for field trips and comments about what is happening in your CA school. Have your child email his teacher friendly notes, not just questions about curriculum, so that he feels connected to the school. (Dan and Marcie Mulligan, PA)

Pace your student so she doesn't become overwhelmed.

Know how to use your CA Scheduler properly. My goal as the Learning Coach is to try my best to cover all the material that is required every day on my daughter's schedule. On a few occasions though, the Scheduler has run three tests on one day. When that happens and my daughter feels too overwhelmed, I just simply run the Scheduler at the end of the day and have one of the tests moved to the next day. On days that the student is sick, you can also run the Scheduler to have everything put back on when she's feeling better. (Beverly Frederick, PA)

The Scheduler guides the Fredericks' learning.

Using Technology

Organize the school day by viewing all your students' schedules simultaneously.

I have three children enrolled and when I log in to my home page I hold down the shift button and click on the Planner icon next to my oldest child's name. That brings up her Planner for the day. I size it to fit into part of the page, and place it on the upper-left-side of the page. (You size the page by clicking and holding the window sizing arrow in the lower right corner of the screen. Just move the mouse and it will make the page smaller or larger, depending on which way you go.) I then hold down the shift button again and click on the Planner icon for my second child. When her page comes up, I size it and place it on the upper-right-side of the page. I then hold down the shift button and click on the Planner icon for my third child. When his page comes up, I size it and place in on the lower-left-side of the page. Now on the lower bar, you can see the pages that are open. Just click on them and they will open up. At that point I have all three Planners visible and am able to see what they need to do for the day. (Toni Schrader, PA)

TIP: Participate in the Connections Academy Message Boards. Not only is this a great way for Learning Coaches to support each other, it's a great way to get to know other's ideas. Use these ideas and grow from them.

Use your Technical Support resources.

Nothing about the LMS system is all that tricky, so if it doesn't work like you think it should, call for help before you get frustrated. Chances are the staff at Tech Support can help you save hours of wondering. They are very knowledgeable and incredibly willing to help. (Barbara Drury, FL)

TIP: Help! Did you ever notice the help icon in the LMS? Just click on it to get additional information.

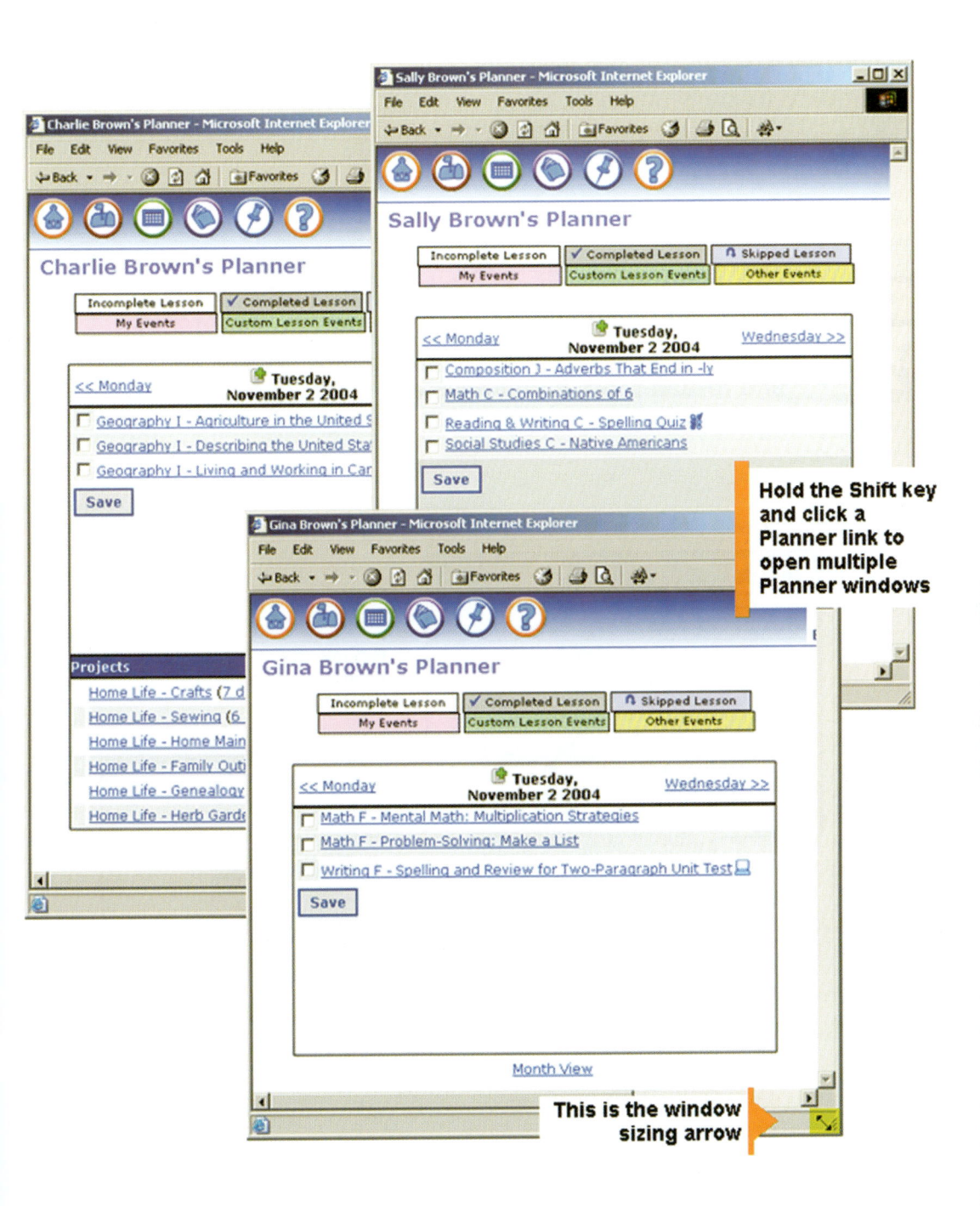

Hold the Shift key and click a Planner link to open multiple Planner windows

This is the window sizing arrow

Using Technology

Review all work before submitting it to the teacher.
Before a student submits an online quiz, be sure they check it. Make sure they know how to click on the exact spot to make sure the answers register properly. (Linda Strathman, CO)

TIP: Make sure you complete the orientation course before you start the school year. You may want to refer to the tutorials again during the year and reread them if you have any questions.

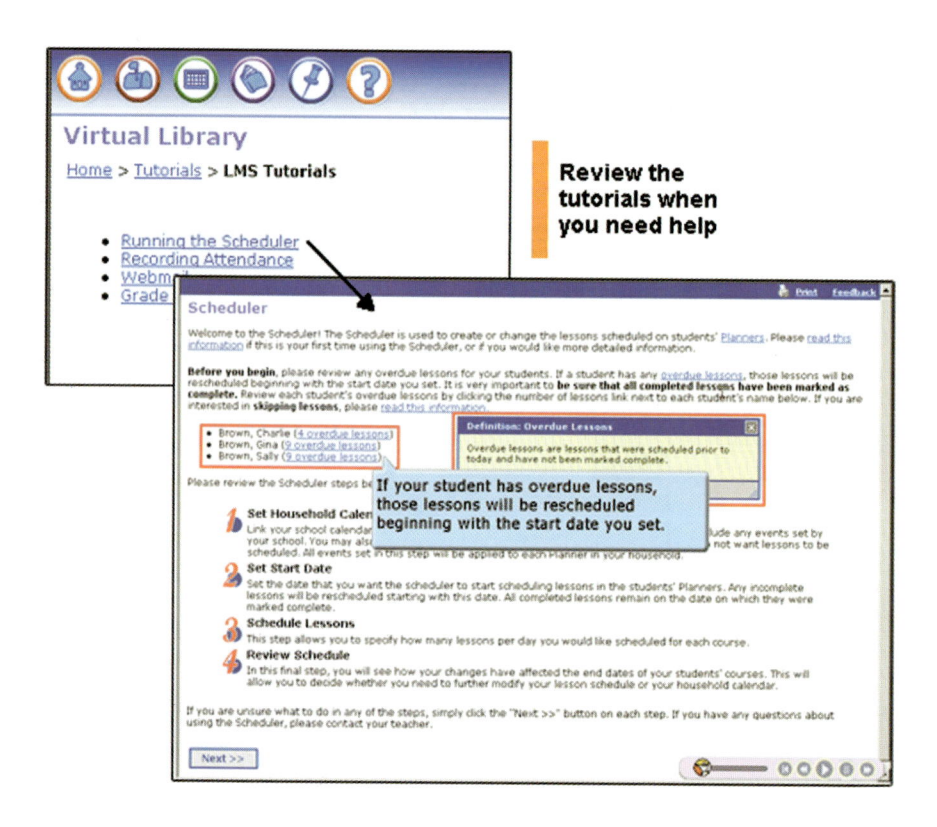

Review the tutorials when you need help

Integrating the Roles of Parent and Coach

Finding ways to integrate the parent and coaching roles can be the biggest hurdle to overcome in a non-traditional setting. Our parents submitted ideas for maintaining composure and staying even-tempered and balanced. Establishing a disciplined and joyful household and integrating household management with coaching are two important keys to success.

Communication is the key to shifting a parent-child relationship to a teacher-student relationship.

Schooling children at home gives parents the opportunity to build on our existing relationships with them. We learn to discipline ourselves and, in turn, we pass this on to our children. Not to sound like a self-help book, but communication is the key to smoothly shifting a parent-child relationship to a teacher-student relationship.

Each year before we start our school program, we talk about the necessary rules and boundaries. It is not uncommon to repeat the rules periodically throughout the year as a reminder. I feel I have to establish these before moving on, or else my daughter could develop the wrong attitude regarding the importance of completing her work at home. The requirements are the same: assignments need to be finished at home just as they are completed at a regular public school.

My standard rules are:

1) Besides being your parent, I am also your teacher. I am here for you to ask me any questions and I will help you the best I can.

2) Breaks are allowed. I don't stick to any certain amount of time or frequency. I usually go by how my daughter is doing and if she is mentally worn out.

(continued)

(continued from previous page)

3) If a lesson proves to be too difficult one day, we can push it off until the next day. It can't get pushed off any more than that or we'll get too far behind.

4) School starts at 8 a.m. For us, it is absolutely imperative that a morning schedule be required just like at a regular "bricks and mortar" school. Our daughter has chosen to get up and start school much earlier than this and I allow it as long as she has had a good breakfast first.

5) Rewards are great as long as the lessons are complete. There were a few occasions where my daughter really needed a break, and incentive to work towards rewards or breaks really motivated her in the long run.

6) No phone calls during lessons, unless they are to or from the teacher.

7) Assess the appropriateness of school Message Boards for your child. For example, you may decide to restrict access for young students. Our family does not use the Message Boards at all. This was our personal choice.*

These seven rules and guidelines set the tone for our entire year. Our daughter knew what was expected of her and that there were clear boundaries and guidelines set from the beginning. (Robyn Jensen, CO)

*Editor's Note: Connections Academy lets you choose whether your students have access to our community message boards or not.

Open communication guides learning for the Jensens.

Keep your cool.
As a parent, I have an emotional investment in my child's education, but I do not have the professional distance that a teacher in a regular classroom environment would have. Keeping my cool can involve counting to ten, changing to a different lesson or simply putting off a lesson until the next day. There are times when I use my son's teacher as support and to back me up. If he doesn't want to do an activity I will have him call the teacher and complain to her, which he doesn't like to do. That usually puts things in perspective. (Becca Gray-Jurek, WI)

TIP: You should make a decision about household chores and stick to it. Some families wait until school is done, while others integrate them into the school day.

Optimize your resources.
My husband and I have split some of the coaching responsibilities. My husband teaches Math, while I cover the other subjects. We've also had another Learning Coach teach the Science curriculum. It has been fun for the boys to experience the different Learning Coaches. (John and Carol Meyer, CO)

Integrating the Roles of Parent and Coach

TIP: Let your students know that you are the Learning Coach (and not so much mom or dad) during the school day.

Create a team atmosphere.

My husband and I often remind the girls that we are all part of "Team Kremer" and that "Team Kremer" needs all of its members working toward a common goal in order to be successful. Sometimes the goal is cleaning the house, sometimes it's getting ready for a trip, sometimes it's trying to get though a school day and sometimes it's being respectful of one another's feelings! We feel it's important for the girls to know that in our home it's not an "us against them" mentality. We are all here to help one another accomplish all that we need to accomplish no matter how big or small a task is and we are all here to support and love one another. (Larry and Nancy Kremer, WI)

Ask for respect.

Being a parent and Learning Coach can be challenging. Keep in mind your child is probably going to test you, especially in the beginning. I always ask for my children to give me the respect that they would give their absolute favorite teacher. (Cheryl Stevens, CO)

Be clear about rules and consequences.

If your child has been in a public school, ask him to tell you some of the rules and start with those, if they are agreeable to your family. Then add more rules pertaining to your own student.

Consequences are an essential tool, especially after a warning or two. Children do well and know they are loved if there are boundaries. Consistent consequences will help them to learn what is expected of them.

If you have a bad day, and you probably will, take time at the end of the day to reflect and think about the needed changes and modifications. (Cheryl Stevens, CO)

Set goals and celebrate successes.

In the beginning of the year, sit down as a family and make a list of positive reasons for using Connections Academy. List how it will enhance your child's education and well-being and the role you all can play in his character formation. During the year when we have achieved successes, we write them down in the same journal. I do this so that when we are ready to pull our hair out, I can reflect upon why we chose to educate at home and the benefit that it is giving us over the long run. It reminds us of the big picture. (Dan and Marcie Mulligan, PA)

A student concentrates on her work.

TIP: Maintain your temper by talking things out with your student when things go wrong. Make sure you are on the same page before you continue.

Extra Credit

When the whole family gets involved, there are many opportunities to make learning fun. Here, our parents share their favorite tips that didn't fit neatly into another category.

Garage sale books spark ideas for the DeLongs.

Use secondhand books to inspire learning.
Cut pictures out of books you find at garage sales, put them in a bag and let the child pick one for inspiration when he can't think of anything to write about in his journal. Use the hardcover on the outside of the book, recover it with material or contact paper and use it to bind the child's written stories. (Tammy DeLong, FL)

Have a Backwards Day!
This is when the day's schedule is reversed and instead of schooling in the morning, we school in the afternoon. The children can choose a Backwards Day at any time as long as it doesn't interfere with the rest of the family's schedule. Sometimes a child just doesn't want to get up early, so he calls for a Backwards Day. (Kim Law, FL)

Communicate regularly with your child's teachers.

At Connections Academy, you have access to a wealth of help and information any time you need it. If your child is struggling, excelling, or having a bad day, communicate that to the teacher. Modifications can be made to help your child, and any information you can provide is important to your child's success. Nothing is too minute or too big to discuss with the teachers or with the principal if the need arises. (Cheryl Stevens, CO)

> **TIP:** Respond to the child's cues and clues. Schedule the day accordingly, and once you notice patterns, make adjustments to the school day routine.

Make sure to build outside activities into your day.

We developed a schedule that allows us to make sure each of our children receives the help he or she needs, and that we have the time to complete the non-school work we need to get done. We build in time during the day for house cleaning and other chores. This gives a much-needed break from school mid-day along with some good exercise.

Sometimes the children complete their assignments before the end of the day. When this occurs, they can work ahead or have some free time for the rest of the day. This became a great motivator for the children to complete their work. Often, they would work ahead so that they could go on a special vacation or an overnight visit with their grandparents or friends. While at first the schedule seemed somewhat confining, in the end it was great for keeping us on track and organizing our time. (Joyce and Jeff Foust, OH)

The Schraders use separate boxes to organize records for each student.

Keep your records together in one place.
I separate records into four categories: enrollment forms and letters, testing and returned Portfolio letters, returned Portfolio work for each child, and curriculum and equipment shipping and packing lists. At the end of the school year, I put each child's returned Portfolio work and completed workbooks into separate boxes and keep them to review over the summer. Then I label them with each child's name, date and grade, and store them. (Toni Schrader, PA)

Try Subject Chunking.
Because of our children's learning styles, we create subject days. We cover Math and Language Arts each day, but we also have a main subject–such as Science, Social Studies, or Geography–that we focus on with two to four lessons per day. This gives us an opportunity to spend more time and concentration on one subject. My children love it, especially when the subject is Art and they get to do more than one project. (Cindy Porter, AZ)

Make learning fun.
We use common games such as bingo to reinforce learning and to prepare for tests. The girls set up their own bingo "cards" with answers and we give them the questions. They cover the answers on their cards until someone has BINGO! (Larry and Nancy Kremer, WI)

Work in pop quizzes.
I work continuously on improving my children's reading comprehension. In addition to the study questions provided by Connections Academy, I thought it would be beneficial to create questions related to each chapter in the book they are reading. I read ahead and after each chapter I create approximately five questions for them to answer. The questions vary in style as well as reading level. Styles can include straight answer, fill-ins, true or false, or short essay. My questions can include a question regarding the setting of the story or who the main character is, or specific details and thoughts about what's going on in the story. This allows me to determine the children's understanding while they exercise their reading comprehension. Additionally, this allows us to have great discussions on the stories. (Lorinda Diaz, FL)

Keep it all together.
Each student has a colored clipboard that has a compartment for storing materials. Inside that compartment, I keep writing paper, drawing paper, pencils and any aids they use (word cards, math tables, punctuation helper). This works well for when we are on the go, as my students always have what they need at their fingertips.

On the top of each clipboard, I print off a list of assignments that we will be doing that day. I also write any reminders on the cover sheet (e.g., remember Drama class at 11:30 a.m.). Under the cover sheet, I place the lesson sheets for that day with highlighted areas. I highlight instruction that I want to include and circle any areas that I expect my students to complete independently. (Amy Riesterer, WI)

TIP: Virtual schooling is a great way to incorporate your values into everyday learning.

Get involved.

Just like anything else, you get out of Connections Academy what you put into it. So get to know your child's teacher. Also get to know other families. We have met many wonderful people who we do things with outside of school. (Kristi and Phil Harms, WI)

The Benton family students enjoy learning together.

Notes

Connections Academy Success Stories

Family Essays

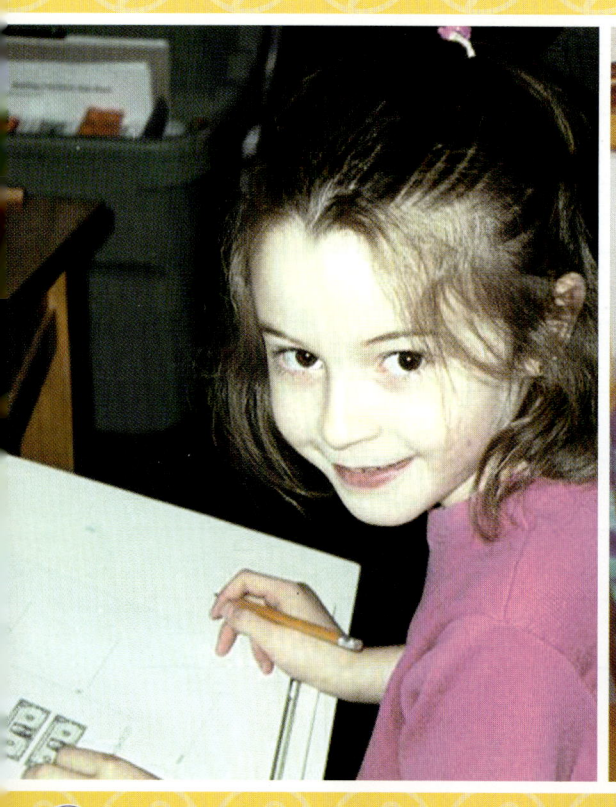

We invited our families to write essays telling us why they chose Connections Academy and what it has meant to them. We heard from many parents who described how their children are thriving in an environment that suits their learning needs with more flexibility, parental involvement, and customized instruction. Each of our families' stories is unique, but they all share the common theme of successful student achievement. Following are six of our favorites.

The Mulligan Family from Pennsylvania

A search for the best school setting for a son born with spina bifida led the Mulligans to Connections Academy. While this condition does not affect his intelligence or learning ability, it does create physical challenges that make a home learning environment ideal.

When my son was ready to attend school, I knew that because he was born with spina bifida, a traditional public school would not be the best choice for him. My plan was to home school him until he could handle his physical limitations, but after the first few years, I realized that he is the type of student who thrives in a home learning environment.

I never believed I would school my son at home beyond the fifth grade, but as he prepared to enter the sixth grade I decided to maintain the home learning environment for him. Although I carefully reviewed curriculum from many companies, I couldn't find anything that challenged him enough, and at the same time encouraged more self-discipline in his studies. I also knew that I needed a program that provided a more thorough and challenging study of his subjects while taking some of the burdens off me.

After researching virtual public schools in my state, I chose Commonwealth Connections Academy. My husband, a public school teacher, and I could not be more pleased with that decision. Connections Academy not only provides an excellent curriculum but also enhances normal studies with weekly assessments so I can make sure my son is grasping what he is being taught. Enrichment lessons encourage him to continue studying the topic in a different way.

We were assigned a fantastic teacher who gave great insight into our educational materials and supported me as a Learning Coach. She has encouraged my son to do the best he can. If I had questions, I was able to call her or email her and she always gave me a quick response. I admire her ability to find answers to my questions that are beyond the assigned lessons and to allow me to speak freely about my opinions and concerns. I am grateful for the encouragement that she gave me, but even more grateful for how she has inspired my son and helped him with his school work.

The biggest bonus of the program has been watching my son enjoy learning more than ever. He has loved the curriculum and the wide array of information it covers. He has a lot of fun using the computer to enhance his studies.

I realized that his knowledge surpassed mine when he proudly did a PowerPoint® presentation about Australia for our family, including his grandfather. He has loved discussing the material that we are reading more than ever because it is presented in such an exciting way. We have had great discussions on topics such as Middle East affairs spurred by a Geography lesson, and whether or not parents should choose the sex of their child from his genetic lessons in Science. He has also developed such a love for writing and has written his own

(continued)

Shakespeare spoof to be played by his friends. This is a direct result of the encouragement that he has received from his teacher and the Language Arts curriculum giving him the necessary tools and structure to complete this project.

My favorite part about Connections Academy is that my son has excitement and enthusiasm about learning, and my husband and I feel the same about teaching him. We are glad that he sees himself as a member of a class of sixth graders with his own teacher. He is thriving in this situation and enjoys being accountable to someone else besides Mom and Dad, while we also enjoy having a higher level of accountability for him.

I am grateful for Connections Academy and everything it has done for my son and his education. It truly has exceeded my expectations. I can't wait for my other two children to be students at Connections Academy as well.

Marcie Mulligan

The Kremer Family from Wisconsin

Despite the fact that they once considered themselves technology phobic, the Kremer family chose the "virtual public school at home" option for their kids. Now using email to communicate with teachers and planning a schedule online is second nature to them.

Our first year at Connections Academy was a very productive one. As the Learning Coaches, my husband and I were responsible for the "hands-on" aspect of teaching our daughters. Our initial trepidation was immediately offset by the wonderful support we received from the Connections Academy teacher and principal.

From the caring support staff and technical help, to the well laid-out curriculum and easy-to-use software, Connections Academy is a top-notch organization that has worked hard to set up successful and innovative virtual schools.

(continued)

Our teacher was only an email away if we ever had a question or concern! It seemed like she always answered our emails within minutes, and if she didn't have an immediate answer, she always followed through. She was patient and kind and wonderful to work with. My daughters really appreciated her phone calls and supportive comments on their homework assignments and tests.

The curriculum is very user-friendly. Not only are the lessons clear and concise, but the plans offer alternatives and teaching tips that are very useful. Seeing the whole month at a glance allows us to effectively plan our time and lessons. The Scheduler is a great tool that permits us to set up a personalized schedule based on our requirements.

Because we definitely are not computer savvy, we were pleasantly surprised (and relieved) at how easy it is to navigate through the software. The few times we did have questions, the capable technical support staff walked us through with patience and professionalism.

Most important to us was the one-on-one time we were able to spend with our girls. We really took the opportunity to make the school year a joint effort. We all learned a lot about each other and it was a joy to see the girls working cooperatively with one another. If one child was having trouble with something, the other would genuinely try to help explain it. The girls were supportive of each other and enjoyed a friendly competition throughout the year. The four of us learned together, laughed together, were perplexed together, figured it out together, and grew closer together!

The girls appreciated the freedom. We had class outside on warm fall and spring days and the girls were able to eat when hungry and work in their pajamas! They were happy not to have traditional homework in the evenings and were glad to be able to start their day at a time of their choosing. All of these perks translated into motivated, enthusiastic kids who had a great school year.

The girls really took responsibility for their learning. Our day was almost always driven by their choices: when to start school, what order to do the classes in, and when to call it a day. We were pleasantly surprised by their stamina and initiative. They totally understood the consequences of procrastination and were almost always the catalysts for getting started in the morning.

As a family we enjoyed a more relaxing year than in the past. We were fortunate not to have the usual tension of a rushing-out-the-door-to-get-to-school morning routine. The girls were able to take advantage of their down time by doing what kids should be doing – just being kids! Their free time was filled with mini-bike riding, family board games, creative art endeavors, imaginative play, and a little more helping around the house. This alone made Connections Academy worth its weight in gold!

We are grateful to have Connections Academy in our lives. Connections Academy is the perfect fit for our family at this time and the girls certainly have continued to blossom in their education. We are proud to have had the courage to take "the road less traveled" and we count our blessings that our lifestyle allows us to be with our children. We are unbelievably fortunate to have a strong, connected, caring family and we are privileged to have been entrusted with caring for two such wonderful children.

Larry and Nancy Kremer

The Stevens Family from Colorado

The Stevens family chose Connections Academy to meet the very different, but equally pressing, learning needs of the two oldest daughters. In a regular classroom, the oldest daughter was seriously struggling; academic setbacks led to low self-esteem, which led to more learning problems – a vicious cycle. The younger sister, on the other hand, mastered concepts quickly but had a difficult time sitting still and focusing. According to mom, both girls have found the Connections Academy curriculum to be an exciting challenge, with the flexibility and professional teacher support they need to thrive.

Connections Academy has been so wonderful and beneficial to my children and me. At Connections Academy, the support that I have received from the staff has been more than a parent could ask for. From the very beginning, they talked with me, helped me, and advised me, but more importantly, they listened to me.

I have a fifth-grader now enrolled in this program, but before we found it she struggled so severely without the help she so desperately needed, that she lacked in self-esteem and self-worth. Through this program and the help and support I received in helping her, she has made a most wonderful turnaround. It has not been easy by any means for either of us, but before Connections Academy I feared losing my child to drugs and other things because of how she felt about herself.

Through Connections Academy and with the appropriate one-on-one attention, I have been afforded the opportunity to show her what she is capable of. Her skill development and self-esteem have taken a tremendous leap.

My second daughter has enjoyed learning and has progressed beyond her peers in a traditional school setting. Since she has a hard time sitting still, this program has been beneficial because of its flexibility. She is proud of what she has learned, as is her older sister.

I am so glad there is a Connections Academy and people who will listen to a parent. I am thankful that they put together a wonderful, beneficial curriculum at a high academic level. This program has far exceeded anything I could have hoped for. The encouragement and dedication of the staff is to be highly commended. I'll bet I learned almost as much as my children. Again, thank you so much for Connections Academy and the most wonderful staff a parent could ask for.

Cheryl Stevens

The Diaz Family from Florida

Since their children both knew how to read by age four, Ceasar and Lorinda Diaz worried about the capacity of their traditional neighborhood school to challenge their children academically. With Connections Academy, they have found the perfect fit for their son and daughter. Connections Academy's Personalized Learning Plan "has allowed the children to accelerate in specific areas, and spend more time on others," Lorinda says.

When we were given the opportunity to learn about Connections Academy, we were excited, yet a bit skeptical. We were excited because it was an alternative to our current situation, but we were doubtful because we were not familiar with the program and not certain if our children would truly enjoy this non-traditional method of learning. After reviewing all the information, we spoke with our children and they were receptive to the idea of attending this new virtual school. After almost a full school year in the program, we have thoroughly enjoyed it and found many benefits. They include a challenging curriculum, a Personalized Learning Plan, and flexibility in learning.

As parents, we wanted to provide our children with the best start and began teaching our children how to read at age four. As a result, both our children were ahead of their grade levels. Connections Academy provides a curriculum that continuously keeps the children challenged. The program has a well-balanced selection of subjects and provides many fun ways of learning which utilize tools via the Internet. We are quite impressed with what the children are learning and even more impressed at how much they enjoy the variety of subjects.

Since our children were ahead of their grade levels, we found the Personalized Learning Plan to be a great benefit to our family. This has provided our children with a curriculum that is customized to their specific needs to get the most out of the learning process. We enjoy the fact that both of our children are given the opportunity to move ahead in subjects they have mastered, but are allowed to be kept in their grade level for other subjects not yet learned.

Since joining Connections Academy, our children are learning more in their average day. They utilize their time more efficiently than in previous years, and the flexibility gives us more time to spend together as a family.

Overall, the Connections Academy program has been tremendously beneficial for us. Our children have improved their writing, reading comprehension, and vocabulary skills. They are exposed to so much more, including Art Appreciation, Music, and Technology and they absolutely love their Science projects. It really makes learning enjoyable when you have the right tools, curriculum, and plan in place.

Ceasar and Lorinda Diaz

The Foust Family from Ohio

This 13-year-old student says the most important thing she learned at Connections Academy is that "it doesn't really matter what grade you get as long as you try your best and really learn what you study." Here she shares the Top 10 reasons why she likes Connections Academy.

I really enjoyed Connections Academy this year and have learned a whole lot from it. I used to just rush through my schoolwork and try to get straight A's, but I really never learned anything I was studying. This year was different because I really learned a lot. There are a ton of reasons why I like Connections Academy. I would like to tell you all of them, but since there are many I'll give you my Top 10:

1) The schedule is very flexible. My family and I really enjoy being able to take vacations when we want. We are able to see and learn a lot of new things.

2) I really enjoy the personal Planner. I can move things up on days when I want to keep studying. Then on other days, I can do fewer lessons and spend time on things like field trips.

3) The teachers are all really nice. I like having the online teachers because if you do not "get" something they will help you. They also call you and email you to see if you understand everything. They even give you really nice compliments if you are doing well on your work.

4) The lessons are really flexible. If you are interested in doing a different Portfolio assignment, you can talk to your teacher to see if you can change it. You can also spread out the work throughout the day.

5) You can do your work at home instead of in a school building. I feel more comfortable doing my work at home. Sometimes, we even do our work outside or at the park.

6) The online assignments are really fun. I really like Technology class and I learned a lot from it. I also like the Music classes because they are neat. It's fun to hear the music on your computer. I like skill-building because you can see how you are doing in school. It also gives really neat tips for doing math problems.

7) The field trips are really awesome. I learned so much at each of them. I think that my favorite field trip was the trip to the Cincinnati Zoo.

8) I like the message boards. It is fun to talk to other kids in my own state and across the United States. I made a bunch of friends from it.

9) I enjoy seeing other Connections Academy students on the field trips.

10) I feel comfortable doing my schoolwork at home. There were a lot of bullies at my other school and I feel safe now.

These are only the Top 10 reasons why I like Connections Academy. Thank you so much for making all this possible for my family and me. You have been a great blessing to all of us.

Foust Family Eighth Grade Student

The Porter Family from Arizona

The Porter family never considered schooling their children at home. But when the events of 9/11 hit too close to home, mom Cindy began looking for an alternative for her previously school-loving daughters.

On September 11, 2001, a terrible event occurred in our country and in our homes. Fear manifests itself in many different ways. I am sure mine is just one of millions of stories, but it is mine just the same.

I am a flight attendant, and have been for over 20 years. My family and I tried to go on as usual after the terror attacks. Unfortunately, my precious little children no longer knew what "normal" was. They would be dropped off at school, only to suffer panic attacks because they felt that mommy was not safe at work. School no longer felt 'safe' anymore. My children's anxiety grew to the point that my daughter's hands were raw and bloody from chewing her nails – the doctor diagnosed it as stress and anxiety. No one should have to be put through such trials, and we felt like we had no alternative. I realized that

I needed to nurture my children myself in order for their fears to be put in check, for them to learn that they are safe, loved, wanted, and precious.

I searched for a school to assist me with our family's goals. I attended an information session for Connections Academy and was overjoyed at what I heard and saw. I immediately enrolled, and my children were thrilled when their curriculum arrived. In a few short weeks my daughter's hands healed and she has not had any problems since.

I must say that all the steps we took as a family have far surpassed our wildest expectations. My "anxious" children are now involved in community sports, church activities, raising animals, and teaching other children about caring for and raising different animals. They sing, they dance, they play. They are children.

Because of my daughter's stress level, she could no longer identify letters, numbers, or written words. Connections Academy allowed us to modify her curriculum, thus saving her pride and feelings of self worth. Now she excels at her work, knows what is expected of her, and rises to the occasion. No competition, no comparing – just pure and joyful learning.

Each of our children is an individual and Connections Academy understands that. The curriculum was tailored to each of their learning levels – not necessarily their "grade" levels. They are able to work at a pace that is comfortable – speeding up over the areas they've mastered and slowing down when something is of particular interest or perhaps more difficult. We also enjoy the contact and feedback from the Connections Academy teachers and staff.

I thank you, my family thanks you, and my heart is grateful to Connections Academy for making what seemed to be impossible possible. I now have happy, confident, smart, and challenged children who can live and learn in an atmosphere of love, trust, and acceptance. To you, I owe my gratitude.

Cindy Porter

Editor's Note: After a year spent at Connections Academy, the Porter children regained their confidence and were able to return to a traditional classroom.

Glossary

Grade Book	A feature of the Learning Management System that allows you to track each student's work progress and monitor performance on an ongoing basis.
Learning Coach	A parent or other responsible adult who implements the Personalized Learning Plan and works in person with the student while collaborating with a certified teacher to deliver instruction. The Learning Coach decides when, where and how to deliver the lessons to create the best possible learning experience for his or her child. Being a Learning Coach requires time, dedication, and a passion to participate in a child's education.
Learning Management System (LMS)	Connections Academy's online tool that students, Learning Coaches and teachers use to communicate with one another, plan and schedule lessons, obtain educational content and assess student performance.
Message Boards	An online discussion forum and medium to distribute school-related information for students and Learning Coaches within the Connections Academy community.

Personalized Learning Plan (PLP)	An individual plan of study prepared by Connections Academy that identifies the strengths and weaknesses of each student and sets appropriate goals and learning strategies.
Planner	A daily, monthly, and school-year calendar that displays scheduled activities for the day.
Portfolio	Work pages, writing assignments, special projects or other student work that is mailed to a teacher for comments and review.
Scheduler	A feature of the Learning Management System that is used to create a personal calendar of lessons and activities for each student.
Virtual School	A school that provides instruction to students outside the traditional classroom, usually at home, guided by qualified teachers from a remote location and facilitated by computers, the Internet, and other communications technology.

Notes